D1613639

Machines at Work

Backhoes

by Cari Meister

Bullfrog
Books

Ideas for Parents and Teachers

Bullfrog Books let children practice nonfiction reading at the earliest reading levels. Repetition, familiar words, and photo labels support early readers.

Before Reading

- Discuss the cover photo. What does it tell them?

- Look at the picture glossary together. Read and discuss the words.

Read the Book

- "Walk" through the book and look at the photos. Let the child ask questions. Point out the photo labels.

- Read the book to the child, or have him or her read independently.

After Reading

- Prompt the child to think more. Ask: Have you ever seen a backhoe? What kind of job was it doing?

Bullfrog Books are published by Jump!
5357 Penn Avenue South
Minneapolis, MN 55419
www.jumplibrary.com

Library of Congress Cataloging-in-Publication Data
Meister, Cari.
  Backhoes / by Cari Meister.
    pages cm. -- (Bullfrog books. Machines at work)
  Includes bibliographical references and index.
  Summary: "This photo-illustrated book for early readers tells about the parts of a backhoe and how the machine is used to put in an underground pipe"-- Provided by publisher.
  Audience: Age 5.
  Audience: Grades K to grade 3.
  ISBN 978-1-62031-042-7 (hardcover : alk. paper) -- ISBN 978-1-62496-054-3 (ebook)
  1. Backhoes--Juvenile literature. 2. Excavation--Juvenile literature. 3. Pipe-laying machinery--Juvenile literature. I. Title.
  TA735.M553 2014
  629.225--dc23   2012042013

Series Editor: Rebecca Glaser
Book Editor: Patrick Perish
Series Designer: Ellen Huber
Book Designer: Sara Pokorny

Photo credits: 123rf, 12–13, 23bl, 24; Dreamstime, 10, 14, 15, 16–17, 23tl, 23tr; iStockphoto, 4, 18, 22; Shutterstock, cover, 1, 3, 5, 6–7, 8, 9, 10–11, 18–19, 21, 23br

Printed in the United States of America at Corporate Graphics in North Mankato, Minnesota.
5-2013 / PO 1003

10 9 8 7 6 5 4 3 2 1

Table of Contents

Backhoes at Work

What can dig
and load?
A backhoe!

A backhoe is digging
a hole to put in a pipe.

6

7

The bucket
has teeth.
It digs.

teeth

The boom moves
the arm.

It goes side
to side.

boom

arm

stabilizer
leg

The strong
stabilizer legs
keep the backhoe
from tipping over.

Look at all the dirt!

It's okay.

It will be used later.

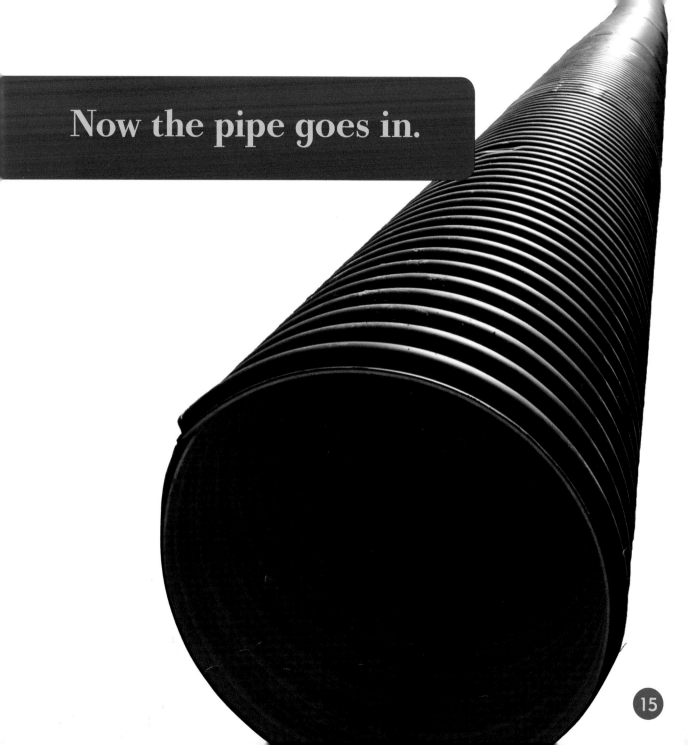

Now the pipe goes in.

The backhoe gets back to work.

The driver has a swivel seat.

He spins to work the other way.

The loader scoops the dirt.
It lifts.
It dumps.
It scoops some more.

loader

Soon the pipe is covered.

The job is done.

Time to go home!

Parts of a Backhoe

boom
The back part of the backhoe's arm that moves side to side.

loader
The backhoe's larger scoop, used mostly for scooping.

bucket
The backhoe's smaller scoop, used mostly for digging.

Picture Glossary

pipe
A metal or plastic tube that carries liquids.

swivel seat
A seat that turns all the way around.

stabilizer legs
The steel legs that rest on the ground and keep a backhoe from tipping over.

teeth
The part of the bucket that tears into the ground.

Index

To Learn More

Learning more is as easy as 1, 2, 3.

1) Go to www.factsurfer.com

2) Enter "backhoe" into the search box.

3) Click the "Surf" button to see a list of websites.

With factsurfer.com, finding more information is just a click away.